The Coding Interview Prep
Handbook was published by
Raydelto Hernandez on
April 30, 2025.

If you find any errors or would
like to contact us for anything,
you can email us at
coding@raydelto.com.

Acknowledgments

I would like to acknowledge the great support that my family and friends have given me throughout the process of writing this book.

Thank you, Roberto Abreu, for your support at every stage of this book's creation. Your help was paramount to the series of events that led to me receiving a job offer as a software engineer at Google, and ultimately, to publishing this book.

Once I announced the release date of this book on LinkedIn, many people showed their support. I am very grateful to all of you for your encouragement on this project, which has been incubating for years.

Foreword

I still remember those 3 AM whiteboard sessions in 2003, sketching graph-traversal logic for our Google Maps–style college project, and watching Raydelto zero in on the "why" behind every line of code. His knack for cutting through complexity with just the right example, never more, never less, was evident even then.

Years later, it made perfect sense when Raydelto handed me the first draft of this book, a straight-to-the-point companion for every aspiring software engineer facing coding interviews. Back in the Dominican Republic, I devoured every programming book I could find, until CLRS, the "bible of algorithms," completely blew my mind. After graduation, I learned there were online programming championships such as "TopCoder," that university students in other countries competed in the International Collegiate Programming Contest (ICPC), and that high-school students competed in the International Olympiads in Informatics (IOI). I had missed out on so much fun. I wanted other students in my country to have these opportunities. Alumni from the ICPC and IOI are very sought after by leading companies. These alumni often change the world. I co-founded the Dominican Olympiads in Informatics

1

(ODI), a national programming contest for high-school students and the bridge to the IOI, and I am the Regional Contest Director (RCD) for the Caribbean at the ICPC. While I'm not in the front lines as a competitor, providing these opportunities gives me the same, if not more, satisfaction.

Over the years, I have seen how many brilliant software engineers get lost in theory or endless question banks. What they really need is a trusted reference, a book that lays out all the necessary data structures and algorithms clearly and concisely, that shows how and when they work. That is exactly what this book provides.

As former fellow Teaching Assistants in our alma mater, tech event organizers, and university instructors in similar subjects, I have witnessed firsthand Raydelto's remarkable ability to teach. His explanations are never longer than they need to be, and they always land. Whether you're reviewing arrays and linked lists, drilling into recursion, or traversing graphs, each chapter will give you the practical knowledge you need in order to succeed.

After reading this book, you will develop effective skills that will help you crush the coding interviews. As you go along, go ahead and practice solving related problems from online platforms. If you get stuck, don't hesitate to come back here. It will contain that easy-to-find, easily digestible piece of programming knowledge you need to get unblocked. Let's get started!

Roberto Abreu
Software Engineer at Meta
Caribbean Regional Contest Director for the ICPC
Director of the Dominican Olympiads in Informatics

1. Introduction

During my professional career as a software engineer at companies such as Google, I have interviewed hundreds of candidates for software engineering positions. In this book, I will teach you everything you need to know to pass the coding interview, a crucial step toward landing your dream job as a programmer. Whether you are seeking your first internship or applying for a role that requires over a decade of experience, you will find value in these pages.

Although the coding interview is a key step toward obtaining a job offer as a Software Engineer, it is not the only component. Be aware that there might be other types of interviews in the recruiting process, like systems design, behavioral and leadership interviews. In this book, I focus exclusively on data structures & algorithms as tools for solving complex problems during your coding interview.

Although it may be part of some coding interviews, we will not cover software engineering topics such as Object Oriented Programming (OOP), design patterns, or design principles.

I have organized the content into two parts: the first (Chapters 2–6) contains context, explanations, and anecdotes that I find relevant to job seeking. However, you can skip this part and jump straight to the second (Chapters 7–19), which covers all the algorithms and data structures chapters of the book.

As the subtitle of the book suggests, my aim is to write a handbook that you can easily read over a weekend and carry around, especially if you still enjoy reading books on paper. To that end, I have focused on only including the steak and leaving out all the fat.

Because of the goals of simplicity, minimalism, and brevity described in the previous paragraph, this book does not include a vast number of coding interview problems. The winning approach to coding interviews is to understand and apply the concepts taught here, rather than memorizing specific problems or patterns. After reading and understanding the content of this book, I recommend practicing these concepts on well-known coding problem-solving platforms such as HackerRank and LeetCode.

The programming language used in this book is C++ (C++17 standard). I chose it over other popular languages in 2025, the year this book was written, because I believe it will remain relevant for decades to come. If I had to bet on which of today's programming languages will still matter in the next decade, I would put my money on C++. It has been a key language since the 1980s and has outlasted multiple waves of so-called C++ killer languages. I know that some Rust and memory safety advocates may disagree, but that is content for another book.

In this book, I focus on algorithms and data structures without delving into the intricacies of any specific programming language. I mostly include function-level code to demonstrate the algorithms, and I use structs when it is necessary to define custom types. Object-oriented programming is not used, and I omit include statements for simplicity. All the code in this book compiles using only a single include statement: *#include <bits/stdc++.h>*, followed by *using namespace std.*

Coding interviews in big tech companies are focused mainly on the two subjects I have mentioned earlier: data structures & algorithms. Because of the influence of big techs on the industry, most companies that hire programmers adhere to the current practices of big tech companies, which make sense, it means to follow the steps of the companies who know what they are doing and consistently deliver strong results.

During the coding interview, make sure to **communicate your thought process out loud at all times**. Avoid a common and significant **mistake**: starting to code before you fully understand the problem and before you have explained your suggested approach, as well as the space and time complexity of your proposed solution. After expressing your intent, explicitly ask your interviewer if it is okay to start coding before you type the first line of code.

The coding interview has evolved during the years. Many years ago, big techs, like Google, used to ask brain teasers during code interviews to measure problem-solving skills, the kind of questions you would get, back in those days, could be something like "How many tennis balls can fit in a school bus". This kind of questions have been vetted, as well as some other topics like dynamic programming. I have written this book with the firm conviction that less is more. In the context of this book, what I mean by using this cliche expression is that by covering less topics, strictly the ones that are most likely to be evaluated in your job interview is more efficient. Instead of writing a heavy book with over six hundred pages, I would rather give you strictly what you need for passing the coding interview, nothing more, nothing less.

All the code in this book can be found in:
https://github.com/raydelto/the-coding-interview

Part 1:

Context.

2. In defense of Coding Interviews

Coding Interviews After the Rise of Artificial Intelligence (AI)

After the launch of ChatGPT by OpenAI in 2022, the world has changed, and so has the field of technical interviews.

Nowadays, we have AI tools that are capable of solving most programming problems used in coding interviews. It is now something that interviewers are actively looking for, to catch cheaters who use AI tools to generate code for them and then claim the authorship.

As of March 2025, some people have claimed to have received job offers from big tech companies like Meta and Amazon by cheating during coding interviews using AI tools.

But the use of AI for cheating purposes is not limited to code generation. Many interviewers have reported that people have used AI tools to alter their webcam feed in order to alter the position of their eyes so that it's not evident that they're getting their answers from another screen that they're not sharing.

It doesn't end there. There have been reported cases of remote interviews where individuals used AI tools to impersonate someone else by altering the video and audio output of their local computers.

Due to the situations described in the previous paragraphs, many articles have been published questioning the value of remote coding interviews today.

In my opinion. Remote work, specifically in the computer programming field, is here to stay.

Undoubtedly, coding interviews have changed due to artificial intelligence. A now common practice during coding interviews includes candidates sharing their screens and displaying all open programs to ensure no AI tools are in use. Furthermore, take-home assignments, once a common evaluation method, have been discontinued. Before the rise of Large Language Models (LLMs), it was standard practice to give candidates an assignment to complete over a few days. However, given the ease with which AI can complete these assignments, their utility has significantly diminished.

The Covid-19 pandemic demonstrated that, in many cases, remote work does not negatively impact productivity, including remote job interviews. Companies like Google and Meta, which traditionally conduct on-site interviews (and still refer to them as such, despite most now being remote), have maintained the remote format due to its significant convenience.

As of 2025, when this book was written, detecting AI filters used to alter video or audio feeds is relatively straightforward. Moreover, while AI can easily generate correct answers to coding problems, a diligent interviewer can readily identify cheaters by asking specific questions about the code they submitted and claimed as their own.

In conclusion, remote coding interviews are here to stay.

Coding Interviews vs. Real Job Tasks

It's widely argued that traditional coding interviews are fundamentally flawed, often requiring candidates to solve problems that bear little resemblance to the day-to-day tasks they would perform if hired.

This criticism, while accurate in its observation, risks overlooking the core objective of technical interviews: to assess a candidate's problem-solving abilities.

Real-world job tasks, often demanding extensive context-specific knowledge and potentially requiring a month or more of training, are simply impractical within the time constraints of an interview. Furthermore, new hires are typically given a significant learning period before being expected to deliver production-ready code.

Beyond simply verifying a candidate's ability to arrive at a correct solution, coding interviews also serve to evaluate their capacity to understand a problem, engage in active listening, and develop efficient solutions. This includes not only consistently producing accurate outputs but also optimizing for memory usage and processing speed. These factors are critical in software development, where performance and resource management are paramount. Moreover, the interviewer can observe the candidate's approach to problem-solving, their communication skills, and their ability to handle pressure, all of which are vital for successful collaboration within a team. Finally, coding interviews help to measure a candidate's ability to learn and adapt to new situations, which is a valuable skill in the ever-evolving field of software engineering.

Therefore, regardless of whether you're applying for a front-end, back-end, full-stack, or niche-specific programming role, coding interviews, as they are currently structured, provide valuable insights. They not only assess your hard skills but also your soft skills. If I have two candidates with equivalent domain-specific knowledge, I would hire the one demonstrating better critical thinking, communication, and decision-making abilities. These soft skills would be more challenging to evaluate if coding interviews were limited to domain-specific, day-to-day tasks.

3. Programmers, Computer Scientists & Software Engineers

The terms Computer Science and Software Engineering are often used as synonyms, but there are important differences between them. Recognizing these distinctions is valuable when preparing for coding interviews.

Computer Science is the study of computers and the principles behind how they perform computations. People in this field are often interested in other scientific disciplines such as mathematics and physics.

Software Engineering focuses on structuring and organizing code in a way that makes it reusable, easy to maintain, and readable. Engineers typically work with broader concerns, including the software development lifecycle, design principles, and design patterns.

I have worked alongside scientists and engineers at several large companies, including Google. Writing code is not limited to computer scientists. Researchers in other fields such as biology, mathematics, physics, and chemistry also write programs to support their work. Today, Python is the most commonly used language for these tasks. In the past, MATLAB was more popular, especially before 2012.

As previously mentioned, both computer scientists and software engineers write code. This means both are considered programmers, which makes *"programmer"* a more general term.

In many cases, it is possible to tell the difference between code written by a computer scientist and code written by a software engineer.

Here are some differences:

1. **Variable names:** Code written by scientists often uses short and non-intuitive variable names. This habit typically stems from their background in mathematics, where it is common to name variables like x, y, z, a, b, or h.

   Engineers, on the other hand, tend to prefer longer but more explicit and intuitive variable names. With modern Integrated Development Environments (IDEs) and code editors, using long variable names does not significantly slow down development, thanks to features like code completion.

2. **Repeated code:** A computer scientist would pay close attention to not having repeated code within a function that will increase the amount of resources needed for producing the expected outcome, but wouldn't mind too much having two different functions with a very similar body structure.

The following table contains popular programmers and their field of study.

Programmer	Field of Study	Known for
Guido van Rossum	Math & Computer Science	Creator of Python
Bjarne Stroustrup	Math & Computer Science	Creator of C++

Richard Stallman	Physics	Creator of GNU
Sergey Brin	Math & Computer Science	Co-Founder of Google
Larry Page	Computer Engineering & Computer Science	Co-Founder of Google
Ilya Sutskever	Math & Computer Science	Former Chief Scientist and Co-founder of OpenAI
Ken Thompson	Electrical Engineering	Co-creator of UNIX & Go.

James Gosling	Computer Science	Creator of Java
Travis Oliphant	Math & Electrical Engineering	Numpy, Scipy
Chris Lattner	Computer Science	Swift,LLVM, Clang, Mojo
Tim Berners Lee	Physics	Creator of the World wide web (WWW)

4. Software Engineer Career Path

Software engineers, often referred to as SWEs, are typically categorized into levels based on their skill and experience. In this chapter, we will outline the most common titles associated with each level.

Please note that for each level, I'll provide a typical range of experience in years. This is not set in stone; it is simply a guideline. It is common to find individuals with decades of experience who never move beyond the Senior Software Engineer role. In many cases, they reach a comfort zone, and their skill level stops progressing.

Entry-Level

This is the first job that a person with no previous experience will land.

The most valuable asset of this first job is the experience that you will attain and add to your resume. Therefore, when you start your first job in the field, if your economic situation allows, try to pick the offer that would give you the most valuable experience, aligned to your areas of interest.

At this point, due to inexperience, you will need close supervision. Therefore, it is uncommon to be able to obtain a remote job at this early stage of your career.

Junior

A junior software engineer has at least one year of experience. At this point you can take on basic programming tasks and on mid-complexity ones with mentorship.

Mid-Level

At this point, you typically have more than two years of experience. You have greater autonomy and can handle tasks of medium complexity with little to no supervision.

Senior

At this level, you have at least four years of experience. You can lead small projects, mentor junior engineers, and make architectural decisions.

This is often the highest position a software engineer can reach in companies where technology is not the core focus. In such environments, this level of expertise is typically sufficient for leading teams, making architectural decisions, handling the company's most complex tasks, and mentoring others.

Staff

At this point, you have at least eight years of experience. You work on complex systems, design software architecture, and influence technical decisions across teams.

Principal

At least twelve years of experience, you're highly experienced, lead major projects and drive company-wide technology strategy.

Distinguished

This rank is hard to obtain, regardless of your years of experience. It is often awarded to recognized experts that have made significant contributions to a field. For instance Kelsey Highttower, one of the biggest contributors to the Kubernetes project is a Distinguished Engineer at Google.

Fellows

This is reserved for elite professionals. For example at Apple, Alan Kay reached the Senior Fellow position for his pioneering work on object-oriented programming and graphical user interfaces.

Regardless of the level of the position you're interviewing for, you will likely be assessed on your ability to solve programming problems involving data structures and algorithms. The complexity of these problems may vary depending on the level of the role.

5. Getting an Interview

Getting invited to a coding interview is the first step toward landing your dream tech job. Regardless of your skill level, you must first catch the attention of a recruiter or hiring manager. Here's a structured approach to help you secure invitations to technical interviews.

Building a Compelling Resume

Your resume is your first impression. Keep these points in mind:

- **Concise and Clear:** Limit your resume to one or two pages. Highlight your most relevant skills, technologies, and experiences.
- **Tailored Content:** Customize your resume for each job posting, aligning your skills and experiences with the specific job requirements.
- **Show, Don't Just Tell:** Use actionable words like "built," "implemented," "optimized," or "led." Include metrics or outcomes to quantify your achievements.
- **Clean Formatting:** Ensure readability with clear headings, bullet points, and consistent fonts and spacing.

Online Presence and Portfolio

A strong online presence can differentiate you from other candidates:

- **LinkedIn Profile:** Maintain an updated LinkedIn profile reflecting your experience, skills, and professional connections.
- **GitHub Contributions:** Regularly commit clean, documented code to your GitHub profile, showcasing personal projects, contributions to open-source projects, or significant achievements.
- **Portfolio Website:** Build a personal website or portfolio highlighting your best projects, contributions, and professional insights.

In 2018, fourteen years after starting my career as a Software Engineer, I got my first job as a Computer Graphics Programming Specialist. Even with over a decade of experience as a SWE, getting a job offer in a highly specialized field like computer graphics programming can be challenging.

In my case, I secured the interview by showcasing my GitHub portfolio, which featured several graphics programming projects I had built on my own. During the interview, the employer asked me detailed questions about those projects to assess my domain-specific knowledge.

What also helped me stand out was the fact that, by then, I had already published a book on the subject. This is another powerful tool to consider. If you have gained expertise in a computer science specialization through personal experimentation and enjoy writing, publishing a technical book can significantly boost your credibility. You can self-publish using Amazon KDP, which is how I published this book.

Alternatively, you can explore traditional publishers like Packt Publishing. They empower subject-matter experts to write books by handling the marketing, editing, and support needed to deliver a polished final product.

I published my first book, *Building Android Games with Cocos2d-x*, with Packt Publishing in 2015. It was a great experience and helped enhance my professional profile.

Networking

Building relationships within the tech industry can dramatically improve your chances:

- **Attend Meetups and Conferences:** Engage with professionals, learn industry trends, and share your expertise.
- **Leverage Alumni Networks:** Connect with alumni who work at companies you are targeting; they might help refer you.
- **Social Media:** Engage in tech communities on platforms like X, Reddit, or specialized forums.

Effective Job Searching

Be strategic about your job applications:

- **Targeted Applications:** Focus on positions closely aligned with your skills and career aspirations.
- **Apply Quickly:** Newer postings typically have fewer applicants, increasing your visibility.
- **Referrals:** Leverage your network to get internal referrals, which significantly increase your chances of landing an interview.

Interacting with Recruiters

Recruiters are gatekeepers to your interview opportunity:

- **Be Professional and Responsive:** Respond promptly and clearly to any recruiter communications.
- **Prepare for Initial Screenings:** Even casual calls or messages from recruiters should be treated professionally. Clearly articulate your skills, interests, and enthusiasm for the role.
- **Follow Up:** Send polite, brief follow-ups if you haven't heard back after two weeks.

Understanding ATS

Many companies use Applicant Tracking Systems (ATS) to filter resumes automatically. Therefore, here are some tricks to help your resume stand out:

- **Keywords:** Include relevant industry terms and technologies directly from the job description.
- **Simple Format:** Avoid elaborate graphics or complex formatting that might confuse ATS systems. Submit your resume in PDF or simple text-based formats for the best compatibility.

Continuous Improvement

Regularly seek feedback and refine your approach:

- **Iterative Process:** Regularly update your resume, online presence, and approach based on feedback and results.
- **Seek Constructive Criticism:** Ask trusted professionals or mentors to review your resume and application materials.

Landing an interview takes strategic preparation, effective networking, and consistent effort. By creating a targeted resume, building a strong online presence, leveraging your network, understanding recruiter interactions, and continuously refining your approach, you'll significantly increase your chances of getting coding interviews.

6. How I Got a Job at Google

On October 22, 2021, I applied for a software engineering position at Google through their careers website.

Just three days later, on October 25, an email from a Google recruiter landed in my inbox, marking the official beginning of my candidacy process. Shortly thereafter, on November 2, another email arrived, this one directly from the recruiter associated with the product area that eventually hired me.

My initial contact with Google's recruiting team took place on November 11, 2021, through a videoconference. During this conversation, the recruiter outlined the recruitment process and provided extensive materials designed to prepare me for the challenging technical interviews ahead. From that moment forward, I dedicated myself entirely to practice data structures, algorithms, and system design principles.

From November 11, 2021, through April 11, 2022, I was immersed in intense, focused study and practice. When I felt ready, on April 11, I promptly informed the recruiter, who immediately responded with an invitation to formally proceed with the interview process.

On April 26, 2022, I faced an intensive sequence of four interviews, called on-site, despite it occurring online. These included one behavioral session, two rigorous coding assessments, and a system design interview.

An encouraging email arrived on May 12, 2022, when the recruiter asked about my availability for a phone call. The very next day, May 13, I received the news I had eagerly anticipated. I had successfully passed Google's challenging interview stages. The recruiter explained that the next step would involve matching my profile with a suitable hiring team within the company.

On May 20, 2022, the recruiter reached out again, letting me know a manager had shown interest in connecting with me. Soon after, on May 23, I had a productive videoconference with the manager of the Software Engineering team within Google's Augmented Reality Hardware group. This conversation was followed closely by another videoconference, held on May 24, with the manager of the Hardware Engineering team in the same area.

On June 7, 2022, I received official confirmation from the recruiter that Google was prepared to extend a job offer, initiating a negotiation phase centered around aligning Google's terms with my career goals and personal circumstances. The negotiation process unfolded smoothly, especially with regard to my request to work remotely from rural New Brunswick, Canada, and my desire to continue teaching at higher education institutions.

Ultimately, Google's formal offer arrived on June 29, 2022, reflecting these considerations. After reviewing the details thoroughly and feeling fully confident in the alignment between Google's goals and my professional aspirations, I officially accepted their offer on June 30.

Finally, on July 25, 2022, my new chapter working at my dream job officially began as I joined Google's Augmented Reality Product Area, stepping into my role as a software engineer on the Hardware Team. This opportunity not only marked a significant career achievement but also affirmed the value of perseverance, meticulous preparation, and clear communication in successfully navigating one of tech's most rigorous hiring processes.

Part 2:

Data Structures & Algorithms

7. Big O Notation

During a coding interview, it is not enough to write code that simply produces the expected output. The interviewer will expect you to provide a solution that optimizes both memory usage (RAM) and processing time.

There are many metrics we could use to evaluate the performance of an algorithm in terms of memory and computational efficiency. However, keep in mind that using execution time as a performance metric is inaccurate, as it heavily depends on the hardware used to run the software. Instead, we aim to isolate the complexity of the software itself.

The metric the interviewer expects you to understand for measuring time and space complexity is Big O notation. This notation describes the computational resources required by an algorithm, in terms of processing time and memory usage in the worst-case scenario.

To illustrate what we mean by worst-case scenario, let's consider the following example of a search algorithm:

Write a function that, given an array of assorted integers and a second integer parameter, returns a boolean indicating whether the second integer is present in the array.

The worst-case scenario occurs when the number the algorithm is searching for is not present in the array. This is because, in order to determine that the number is not contained, the algorithm must perform the maximum number of operations by checking every element before concluding that the number was not found.

Big O notation expresses an algorithm's complexity in terms of the size of the input, often referred to as **N**.

An algorithm with a time complexity of **O(N)** means that, in the worst-case scenario, the number of steps it performs is proportional to the number of inputs provided.

From a space point of view, a space complexity of O(N) means that the amount of memory required to execute the algorithm grows at a linear rate relative to the input size.

Returning to our earlier search problem: if we implement a **linear search** algorithm, which traverses each position in the array and checks whether it contains the target number, then, as mentioned earlier, if the number is not in the array, the algorithm must examine each element. Therefore, the number of steps it performs is equal to the size of the array. This type of complexity is called **linear complexity**, and in Big O notation, it is written as **O(N)**.

Now that you understand how Big O notation works, let's look at other common complexities you may encounter during your interview.

Quadratic complexity (O(N²)): As you might expect, this type of complexity means that, from a time standpoint, the number of steps the algorithm performs is proportional to the square of the input size. You can easily identify a quadratic algorithm by noticing a nested loop operating on the input parameter.

The following bubble sort implementation is an example of an algorithm with a complexity of **O(N²)**:

```cpp
void bubbleSort(vector<int>& arr) {
  int size = arr.size();
  bool swapped;

  // Perform n-1 passes
  for (int i = 0; i < size - 1; ++i) {
    swapped = false;

    // Compare adjacent elements
    for (int j = 0; j < size - i - 1; ++j) {
      if (arr[j] > arr[j + 1]) {
        swap(arr[j], arr[j + 1]);
        swapped = true;
      }
    }

    // If no swaps, the array is sorted
    if (!swapped)
      break;
  }
}
```

Cubic complexity (O(N^3)): As you might guess by now, an algorithm with this type of complexity can typically be identified by a loop with two additional levels of nested loops. The number of steps required for such an algorithm to produce a result is proportional to the cube of the input size. This level of complexity is generally inefficient and should be avoided if possible.

If you arrive at a solution with cubic complexity during a coding interview, there's a good chance that a more efficient approach can be implemented.

The following code listing shows a naïve solution to the common **3-Sum** problem:

Problem Statement: Given an array of integers, find all unique triplets (a,b,c) such that $a + b + c = 0$ and a, b and c are distinct elements:

```cpp
vector<vector<int>>
findTripletsBruteForce(vector<int>& nums) {
  vector<vector<int>> result;
  set<vector<int>> uniqueTriplets;

  int n = nums.size();
  if (n < 3) {
    return result;   // Not enough elements
  }

  for (int i = 0; i < n; ++i) {
    for (int j = i + 1; j < n; ++j) {
      for (int k = j + 1; k < n; ++k) {
        if (nums[i] + nums[j] + nums[k] == 0) {
          vector<int> triplet(3);
          triplet[0] = nums[i];
          triplet[1] = nums[j];
          triplet[2] = nums[k];
          sort(triplet.begin(), triplet.end());
          uniqueTriplets.insert(triplet);
        }
```

```
        }
      }
    }
  return result;
}
```

Logarithmic complexity (O(log N)): This is considered a very good algorithmic complexity. If you come up with a solution of this kind during your interview, chances are you did well. While it is not the absolute best in terms of performance, it is still highly efficient because the number of steps increases very slowly compared to the size of the input.

A common example of an algorithm with logarithmic complexity is **binary search**. Given a sorted list, this algorithm repeatedly divides the list in half. If the target number is greater than the largest number in the left half, all elements in that half can be discarded, and the search continues in the right half. With each step, half of the remaining elements are eliminated.

For example, imagine an input list with 1,000,000 elements. In just one step, binary search can discard 500,000 elements. It would take only 20 steps to determine that a number is not present in a sorted list of that size. In contrast, a linear search could require up to 1,000,000 steps to reach the same conclusion.

That makes it 50,000 times slower for this particular case!

In Chapter 9 (Array Search Algorithms), I will cover the binary search algorithm.

Log-linear complexity (O(N log N)): This is another common algorithmic complexity. It represents a combination of a linear and a logarithmic algorithm.

An example of a log-linear complexity algorithm is **merge sort**. This sorting algorithm consists of two main steps: repeatedly splitting the input into halves and sorting each half. The splitting step has a complexity of **O(log N)**, while the sorting step has a complexity of **O(N)**.

O(N log N) is the best possible Big O complexity for a general-purpose sorting algorithm. This is because, regardless of the technique used, if we want to sort all elements in an array, the algorithm must process each element at some point.

Constant complexity (O(1)): This is the most efficient type of algorithm. It means that the number of steps required to produce an output is independent of the size of the input. A simple example would be an algorithm that prints the first element of a list.

Regardless of the list's size, it takes the same amount of effort to produce the output.

A classic constant-time algorithm example is the retrieval operation of a hash map. Regardless of the size of the map, it can return the value associated with a given key by creating a numeric representation of the key, allowing quick access to its associated value.

8. Arrays & Strings

Arrays and strings are among the simplest data structures covered in the material you will be evaluated on. Despite their simplicity, it is very likely that at least one of the coding problems you encounter in your interview will involve them

To keep things clear and ensure that we are all starting from the same point, let's review the basics of arrays before moving forward.

1. In memory, arrays are laid out in contiguous space, allowing constant-time access, or **O(1)**.
2. Array indices begin at 0.
3. The last index of an array is its size minus one.
4. One limitation of arrays is that they are best suited for situations where you know in advance how many elements you want to store. While it is possible to handle dynamically growing data with arrays, doing so typically requires copying the entire array into a new one whenever the current buffer is full. This process is computationally expensive.

Array Performance Optimizations

Single-dimensional arrays: Low-level APIs such as OpenGL always use single-dimensional arrays, even for representing matrices.

The reason for this is that it is faster for the CPU to retrieve contiguous bytes from RAM, which is always the case with single-dimensional arrays.

When we use a two-dimensional array, what we effectively have in RAM is a one-dimensional array in which each element holds the address of another one-dimensional array. This means that each row of the two-dimensional array resides at a separate memory location. Accessing non-contiguous memory addresses for each row introduces additional overhead and can negatively impact performance.

To avoid this, it is common to represent the matrix as a single-dimensional array and manually calculate the row and column indices. This way, the element at position *(i, j)* in a matrix can be accessed using a formula like array[i * num_columns + j], which leverages contiguous memory and improves efficiency.

Example:

Let's say that we would like to store the following 3x3 matrix:

1   2   3

4   5   6

7   8   9

We could store these numbers in a single array, and then access to the representation of the two-dimensional matrix as follows:

```cpp
int getElement(const vector<int>& matrix,
               int row, int col,
               int numCols) {
  return matrix[row * numCols + col];
}
```

That said, always prioritize **readability** and **correctness** over premature optimization. Let the interviewer know that you are aware of the performance implications of using two-dimensional arrays, but ask if it is acceptable to use them for the sake of clarity during the interview. Chances are they will say yes, as they are more interested in evaluating your ability to solve the overall problem efficiently and correctly.

In this book, I will cover many algorithms that involve the use of arrays and strings.

In the next chapter, array search algorithms will be covered."

9. Array Search Algorithms

In this chapter, I will cover search algorithms that can be used within array data structures. These algorithms form the core of many coding interview problems.

Common search algorithms include linear search and binary search.

Linear Search

Linear search sequentially checks each element in a dataset until the target element is found or the list ends. To be clear, in most cases, linear search is not considered an efficient solution.

Complexity: O(n)

```cpp
int linearSearch(const vector<int>& arr,
                 int target) {
  for (int i = 0; i < arr.size(); ++i) {
    if (arr[i] == target)
      return i;
  }
  return -1;  // not found
}
```

Binary Search

Binary search efficiently finds an element in a sorted array by repeatedly dividing the search interval in half.

Complexity: O(log n)

```cpp
int binarySearch(const vector<int>& arr,
                 int target) {
  int left = 0, right = arr.size() - 1;

  while (left <= right) {
    int mid = left + (right - left) / 2;

    if (arr[mid] == target)
      return mid;
    if (arr[mid] < target)
      left = mid + 1;
    else
      right = mid - 1;
  }
  return -1;  // not found
}
```

10. Linked Lists

After covering arrays, the natural next topic is linked lists.

A linked list is a data structure in which each node contains a pointer to the memory address of the next element in the list. Because of this basic design, a linked list does not require contiguous memory allocation and can therefore use memory more efficiently than an array in some scenarios.

One of the main limitations of arrays is their inefficiency when handling dynamically growing data. This is where linked lists offer a clear advantage. Adding a new element to a linked list has a constant time complexity of $O(1)$, and linked lists generally use less memory for dynamically allocated data because, unlike arrays, they do not require preallocating buffer space.

The downside of linked lists is their linear time complexity, $O(N)$, for accessing a given index, which is significantly worse than the constant-time, $O(1)$, read access provided by arrays.

There are primarily two types of linked lists:

- **Singly Linked List:** Elements point only forward.
- **Doubly Linked List:** Elements point both forward and backward.

Both singly and doubly linked lists can be <u>circular</u> if the last element points to the first element. In a doubly linked circular list, the first element also points back to the last element as its previous node. An example of a circular list is a music playlist where the user has enabled the *repeat all* option.

Implementing a Doubly Linked List

Let's start by manually implementing a doubly linked list in C++:

```cpp
struct Node {
    int data;
    Node* next;
    Node* prev;

    Node(int value) : data(value),
                      next(nullptr),
                      prev(nullptr) {}
};
```

```cpp
struct DoublyLinkedList {
  Node* head;
  Node* tail;
  DoublyLinkedList() : head(nullptr),
                       tail(nullptr) {}

  void append(int value) {
    Node* newNode = new Node(value);
    if (head == nullptr) {  // Is empty
      head = newNode;
    } else {
      tail->next = newNode;
      newNode->prev = tail;
    }
    tail = newNode;
  }

  void prepend(int value) {
    Node* newNode = new Node(value);
    if (tail == nullptr) {  // Is empty
      tail = newNode;
    } else {
      newNode->next = head;
      head->prev = newNode;
    }
    head = newNode;
  }
```

```cpp
void deleteNode(int value) {
  Node* current = head;
  while (current != nullptr) {
    if (current->data == value) {
      if (current->prev != nullptr)
        current->prev->next =
                    current->next;
      else
        head = current->next;

      if (current->next != nullptr)
        current->next->prev =
                    current->prev;
      else
        tail = current->prev;

      delete current;
      return;
    }
    current = current->next;
  }
}

void displayForward() const {
  Node* current = head;
  while (current != nullptr) {
    cout << current->data << " ";
    current = current->next;
  }
```

```cpp
      cout << endl;
    }

    void displayBackward() const {
      Node* current = tail;
      while (current != nullptr) {
        cout << current->data << " ";
        current = current->prev;
      }
      cout << endl;
    }
};
```

Leveraging C++'s Standard Library (std::list)

C++ provides an efficient and robust implementation of a doubly linked list through *std::list* from the standard library. Among other features, it includes functions such as *push_back*, *push_front*, *pop_back*, *pop_front*, and *splice* (for moving elements from one position to another). It also provides access to the front and back elements.

std::list maintains a linked structure of nodes, and iterators provide an abstraction to traverse and manipulate these nodes.

This implementation provided in the C++ standard library is sufficient for most interview problems that involve a linked list. Ask your interviewer whether it is acceptable to use this implementation or if they would prefer that you implement your own. Depending on the position you are applying for, they might require a custom implementation to assess your understanding of low-level memory management.

Here is an example use of std::list:

```cpp
int main() {
  list<int> numbers;


  numbers.push_back(1);
  numbers.push_back(2);
  numbers.push_front(3);

  cout << "List elements: ";
  for (int num : numbers) {
    cout << num << " ";
  }
  cout << endl;

  // Removing elements
  numbers.remove(1);
```

```cpp
    cout << "After removal: ";
    for (int num : numbers) {
      cout << num << " ";
    }
    cout << endl;

    // Reversing the list
    numbers.reverse();
    cout << "After reverse: ";
    for (int num : numbers) {
      cout << num << " ";
    }
    cout << endl;

    return 0;
}
```

Output:

```
List elements: 3 1 2
After removal: 3 2
After reverse: 2 3
```

11. Two-Pointer Technique

The two-pointer technique is commonly used for solving arrays and linked lists problems. It leverages the idea of maintaining two pointers, or indices, that move through the data structure, often in a coordinated manner. This technique can significantly improve the time complexity of your solutions, often reducing it from $O(N^2)$ or higher to $O(N)$.

The premise is the following: instead of using nested loops to compare every element with every other element, use two pointers to traverse the data structure. The way these pointers move and the conditions under which they change depend on the specific problem.

Common Scenarios:

- **Finding pairs:** Finding pairs of elements that satisfy a certain condition (e.g., sum to a target).
- **Reversing arrays or lists:** Reversing the order of elements efficiently.
- **Finding middle elements:** Locating the middle element of a linked list.
- **Detecting cycles:** Determining if a linked list contains a cycle.

- **Partitioning arrays:** Rearranging elements based on a specific criterion.
- **Merging sorted arrays or lists:** Combining two sorted sequences into a single sorted sequence.

Types of Two-Pointer Approaches

Let's explore the common variations of the two pointers technique:

Moving in Opposite Directions

In this scenario, one pointer starts at the beginning and the other at the end, and they move toward each other until they meet.

This is often used for problems like reversing an array or finding pairs with a specific sum in a sorted array.

Another coding problem you could solve using this approach is detecting palindromes, which are strings that read the same backward and forward. You can compare both pointers (start and end), and if they contain different characters at any point, return false.

Moving in the Same Direction

This approach is known as **Sliding Window**. This is commonly used for problems involving finding subarrays or subsequences that satisfy a certain condition.

Both pointers move in the same direction, but one may move faster than the other, creating a *window* of elements. The next chapter is dedicated to this specific case of the two-pointer technique.

Fast and Slow Pointers

This technique,commonly known as *Tortoise and Hare*, is primarily used for linked list problems, particularly for cycle detection and finding the middle element. In such cases, one pointer moves at a faster pace than the other.

Example 1: Finding Pairs with a Given Sum (Two Sum Array).

Problem: *Given a sorted array of integers in ascending order and a target sum, determine whether there exists a pair of elements in the array whose sum equals the target.*

```cpp
bool findPairSum(const vector<int>& numbers,
                 int targetSum) {
  int left = 0;
  int right = numbers.size() - 1;

  while (left < right) {
    int currentSum =
           numbers[left] + numbers[right];

    if (currentSum == targetSum) {
      return true;
    } else if (currentSum < targetSum) {
      left++;
    } else {
      right--;
    }
  }

  return false;
}
```

Explanation:

1. We initialize two pointers, *left* and *right*, at the beginning and end of the array, respectively.
2. We calculate the sum of the elements pointed to by left and right.
3. If the sum equals the target, we return true.
4. If the sum is less than the target, we increment left to consider a larger element.

5. If the sum is greater than the target, we decrement *right* to consider a smaller element.
6. We repeat steps 2-5 until left and right cross each other.

Example 2: Reversing an Array

```cpp
void reverseArray(vector<int>& arr) {
    int left = 0;
    int right = arr.size() - 1;

    while (left < right) {
        swap(arr[left], arr[right]);
        left++;
        right--;
    }
}
```

Explanation:

1. Initialize left and right pointers to the start and end of the array.
2. Swap the elements at left and right.
3. Increment left and decrement right.
4. Repeat until left crosses right.

Example 3: Detecting a Cycle in a Linked List (Fast and Slow Pointers)

```cpp
struct ListNode {
  int val;
  ListNode* next;
  ListNode(int x) : val(x),
                    next(nullptr) {}
};
bool hasCycle(ListNode* head) {
  if (head == nullptr ||
      head->next == nullptr) {
    return false;
  }

  ListNode* slow = head;
  ListNode* fast = head->next;

  while (fast != nullptr &&
         fast->next != nullptr) {
    if (slow == fast) {
      return true;
    }
    slow = slow->next;
    fast = fast->next->next;
  }

  return false;
}
```

Explanation:

1. Initialize slow and fast pointers. slow moves one step at a time, and fast moves two steps.
2. If there's a cycle, fast will eventually catch up to slow.
3. If fast reaches the end of the list (nullptr), there's no cycle.

Practice Problems

Remember, to excel in coding interviews, you need to practice. The more you practice, the more knowledge you add to your problem-solving toolkit. The following LeetCode problems will help you reinforce the concepts introduced in this chapter.

- Two Sum II - Input Array Is Sorted (LeetCode 167)
- Reverse String (LeetCode 344)
- Linked List Cycle (LeetCode 141)
- 3Sum (Leetcode 15)
- Container With Most Water (LeetCode 11)

The two-pointer technique is a fundamental tool in your coding interview arsenal. Mastering its variations and understanding when to apply it will lead to efficient and elegant solutions for a wide range of problems. Remember to analyze the problem carefully and choose the appropriate pointer movement strategy. By practicing these examples and tackling the practice problems, you will gain confidence in using this powerful technique.

The next chapter is exclusively dedicated to the **sliding window** two-pointer technique.

12. Sliding Windows

As we saw in the previous chapter, the sliding window is a common case of the two-pointer technique. It is used to solve problems involving subarrays or substrings. This method reduces redundant computations by maintaining a subset of data (the "window") and dynamically adjusting its boundaries as the algorithm progresses.

A sliding window algorithm typically involves two pointers or indices representing the left and right boundaries of the window. The window expands and contracts based on specific conditions, allowing problems to be solved in linear time complexity.

When to Use Sliding Window

- Finding subarrays or substrings meeting certain criteria (e.g., maximum/minimum sum, specific length, containing unique elements).
- Problems involving contiguous sequences or intervals within arrays or strings.

Example: Maximum Sum of a Fixed-Size Subarray

Given an array of integers *nums* and an integer *winSize*, find the maximum sum of any contiguous subarray of size *k*.

```cpp
int maxSumSubArray(const vector<int>& nums,
                   int winSize) {
  int windowSum = 0;
  int maxSum = numeric_limits<int>::min();

  for (int i = 0; i < nums.size(); ++i) {
    windowSum += nums[i];

    if (i >= winSize - 1) {
      maxSum = max(maxSum, windowSum);
      windowSum -= nums[i - (winSize - 1)];
    }
  }

  return maxSum;
}
```

If you analyze the code above, you will notice that we have reduced the number of steps required to calculate the *windowSum* value by simply adding the next element on the right-hand side of the window and subtracting the leftmost one. This approach avoids recalculating the sum of each window from scratch every time we move, which would otherwise result in duplicated effort.

Example: Longest Substring of Repeating Characters

Given a string s, return the length of the longest contiguous substring that contains only repeated instances of a single character.

```
int longestRepeating(const string& s) {
  if (s.empty())
    return 0;

  int maxLen = 1;
  int start = 0;

  for (int end = 1; end < s.length(); ++end) {
    if (s[end] != s[start]) {
      start = end;
    }
    maxLen = max(maxLen, end - start + 1);
  }

  return maxLen;
}
```

Notice that we add 1 when calculating maxLen. This is because array indices start at 0, and we are calculating the length of a substring.

Advantages of Sliding Window

The sliding window two-pointer technique offer these advantages:

- **Efficiency**: Achieves linear time complexity (O(N)) by avoiding redundant computations.
- **Simplicity**: Clear logic makes algorithms easier to implement and understand.

13. Queues

Queues manage collections of elements in a First-In-First-Out (FIFO) manner. They play a crucial role in solving various coding interview problems, especially those involving task scheduling, breadth-first tree traversals, or request management in simulations.

In a queue, elements are added (enqueued) at the rear and removed (dequeued) from the front. This ensures that the first element inserted into the queue is the first to be removed.

Standard Queue Operations

enqueue (push): Add an element to the rear of the queue.

dequeue (pop): Remove and return the front element of the queue.

front: Access the front element without removing it.

empty: Check if the queue is empty.

Queue operations for add (*push*) and retrieve (*front*) element have a constant time complexity O(1).

Queue Implementation in C++

The Standard Template Library (STL) in C++ provides a convenient queue implementation. The following code demonstrates its usage:

```cpp
int main() {
  queue<int> q;

  q.push(10);  // enqueue
  q.push(20);
  q.push(30);

  while (!q.empty()) {
    cout << q.front() << " ";
    q.pop();  // dequeue
  }

  return 0;
}
```

Output:

```
10 20 30
```

Types of Queues

Summary

For coding interview purposes, the following are the two most relevant types of queues:

Simple Queue (queue): Basic First-In-First-Out (FIFO) structure.

Priority Queue (priority_queue): Elements removed based on priority rather than insertion order.

Simple queues

Overall, simple queues are data structures that provide a mechanism for retrieving its first element in linear time and removing it after performing a given operation."

In Chapter 19, where we cover the graph data structure, we are going to use simple queues to perform breadth-first searches, which are the recommended type of search for finding the shortest path between two given vertices.

Priority queues

Priority queues allow you to keep data sorted in ascending or descending order at all times.

The following code demonstrates C++ STL implementation of priority queues.

```cpp
int main() {
  priority_queue<int, vector<int>,
        greater<int>> ascending;
  priority_queue<int> descending;
  vector<int> values = {10, 20, 5, 30};

  // Add values to each priority queue
  for (const int& value : values) {
    ascending.push(value);
    descending.push(value);
  }

  cout << "Ascending order: ";
  while (!ascending.empty()) {
    cout << ascending.top() << " ";
    ascending.pop();
  }
  cout << endl;

  cout << "Descending order: ";
  while (!descending.empty()) {
```

```
    cout << descending.top() << " ";
    descending.pop();
  }
  cout << endl;
}
```

Output:

```
Ascending order: 5 10 20 30
Descending order: 30 20 10 5
```

For any problem statement that requires you to have quick access to the minimum of maximum value, you can use a priority queue.

Example: Connect Ropes with Minimum Cost

Problem Statement:

You are given *n* ropes with different lengths. Your task is to connect all the ropes into one single rope. The cost of connecting two ropes is equal to the sum of their lengths.

You can only connect two ropes at a time. Find the minimum total cost to connect all the ropes.

Solution:

```cpp
int minimumCost(const vector<int>& lengths) {
  priority_queue<int, vector<int>,
        greater<int>> ropes;
  for (int len : lengths) {
    ropes.push(len);
  }

  int totalCost = 0;

  // Keep combining the two shortest ropes
  while (ropes.size() > 1) {
    int first = ropes.top();
    ropes.pop();
    int second = ropes.top();
    ropes.pop();

    int cost = first + second;
    totalCost += cost;

    ropes.push(cost);
  }

  return totalCost;
}
```

```
Input:    {4, 3, 2, 6}
Output: Minimum total cost: 29
```

14. Stacks

Stacks follow the Last-In-First-Out (LIFO) principle, meaning the most recently added element is the first to be removed. They are used in problems, such as expression evaluation and syntax parsing.

Elements in a stack are added and removed from the top, ensuring the last inserted element is always accessed first.

Standard Stack Operations

push: Add an element onto the stack.

pop: Remove the top element from the stack.

top: Access the top element without removing it.

empty: Check if the stack is empty.

All of the above operations have a constant time complexity $O(1)$.

Stack Implementation in C++

The Standard Template Library (STL) provides a stack implementation. Here, we present a simple example of how to use it.

```cpp
int main() {
    stack<int> s;

    s.push(10);
    s.push(20);
    s.push(30);

    while (!s.empty()) {
        cout << s.top() << " ";
        s.pop();
    }
}
```

Output:

```
30 20 10
```

Applications of Stacks

Expression Evaluation: Evaluating arithmetic expressions.

Syntax Parsing: Matching parentheses, braces, and brackets.

Undo Operations: Tracking previous states or actions.

Example: Check parentheses syntax

Given an expression determines if the parentheses syntax is, i.e. all opened parentheses are closed, and there are no closed parentheses without a matching open parentheses.

Test cases:

```
((1+2)/(3+4))*6  -> true
)3(2+2) *2 -> false
```

Solution:

```cpp
bool isValid(const string& expr) {
  stack<char> buffer;

  for (char ch : expr) {
    if (ch == '(') {
      buffer.push(ch);
    } else if (ch == ')') {
      if (buffer.empty() ||
          buffer.top() != '(') {
        return false;
      }
      buffer.pop();
    }
  }
  return buffer.empty();
}
```

The code above iterates through the string. If an opening parenthesis is found, it is added to the stack. If a closing parenthesis is found, we check whether the element on top of the stack is an opening parenthesis; if it is not, we return false. At the end, we return the result of calling buffer.empty(), because if the stack is not empty after traversing the entire string, it means the expression is incorrect.

You might have noticed that this is a simplified example, and that we are only adding opening parentheses to the stack. Therefore, the if statement that checks whether the element on top of the stack is '(' is always going to return true as long as the stack is not empty.

This over-simplification was done on purpose. Now, you get to modify the code to add support for other mathematical expression grouping symbols.

15. Maps

Maps are versatile and frequently used data structures, providing efficient storage and retrieval of key-value pairs. The C++ Standard Template Library (STL) offers two primary types of maps: ordered maps (*map*) and unordered maps (*unordered_map*). Each type serves different purposes, has different implementations, and thus different time complexities.

Ordered Maps

An ordered map in C++ (*map*) maintains its elements sorted according to the keys in ascending order.

Performance:

- Insertion: O(log n)
- Lookup: O(log n)
- Deletion: O(log n)

The main reasons to use an ordered map instead of an unordered one are when you need to keep the keys sorted or perform prefix or range-based queries. This comes at a significant time complexity cost, as unordered maps offer average constant-time complexity O(1) for insertion and retrieval operations, which is significantly faster than the logarithmic complexity O(log n) of ordered maps.

Unordered Maps

Unordered maps (*unordered_map in C++*) are hash based structures. They provide extremely fast average-time complexity for insertion and lookup operations. However, they do not maintain keys in any particular order.

Performance:

- Insertion: $\Theta(1)$
- Lookup: $\Theta(1)$

For the first time in this book, these time complexities are given in terms of the average case (Θ) rather than the worst-case scenario (O). In the worst-case scenario, where all keys produce the same hash, insertion and lookup operations will have linear time complexity O(N).

Use unordered maps when order is not important and you require the best average performance for key-value retrieval and insertion.

The problem you will be asked to solve during the coding interview will most likely be suitable for an unordered map. However, pay close attention, and if it is not completely clear, ask your interviewer whether storing the keys in sorted order is required.

As an example, we are going to solve the commonly known interview problem Two Sum, which we saw in the Sliding Window chapter (Chapter 12), this time using an unordered map.

<u>Problem Statement:</u>

Given an array of integers *nums* and an integer *target*, return the indices of the two numbers such that they add up to target.

Solution:

```cpp
vector<int> twoSum(const vector<int>& nums,
                   int target) {
  // Map to store value -> index
  unordered_map<int, int> mappedValues;

  for (int i = 0; i < nums.size(); ++i) {
    int complement = target - nums[i];

    // Check if the complement exists
    if (mappedValues.find(complement) !=
                      mappedValues.end()) {
      return {mappedValues[complement], i};
```

```
    }

    // Store current index
    mappedValues[nums[i]] = i;
  }

  // No solution found
  return {};
}
```

Memoization

No, there is no typo. *Memoization* is a computer science term that refers to storing the results of previous computations to avoid redundant work.

Because maps provide a key-value pair mechanism, they are a good choice for storing the results of previous computations.

In our recursion chapter, we will use maps to implement the memoization technique and avoid repeating computations.

16. Sets

Sets store unique elements and provide efficient ways to manage collections where duplicates are not allowed. Like maps, C++ offers two main types of sets in its Standard Template Library (STL): ordered sets (set) and unordered sets (unordered_set).

Ordered Sets

An ordered set in C++ (set) ensures that elements are always sorted in ascending order by value.

Performance:

- Insertion: $O(\log n)$
- Lookup: $O(\log n)$
- Deletion: $O(\log n)$

Ordered sets are ideal when you need sorted storage, quick access to elements in order, or a predictable worst-case performance.

Unordered Sets

Unordered sets (unordered_set) are hash-based structures that offer constant $O(1)$ average-time complexity for insertion, deletion, and lookup, without maintaining any particular order of elements.

Performance:

- Average-case insertion, deletion, and lookup: $\Theta(1)$
- Worst-case insertion, deletion, and lookup: $O(n)$

Similarly, as we saw in the previous chapter about maps, we use average-case Θ notation because unordered sets provide constant-time performance in the average case $\Theta(1)$ for insert and retrieval operations. In rare edge cases where the hash function produces the same value for all elements, the time complexity becomes linear $O(N)$.

Unordered sets are perfect when performance is critical and element ordering is not required.

Example problem:

Given an integer array *nums*, return a boolean value indicating whether or not it contains duplicate values.

Can you solve it yourself? The solution is on the next page.

Solution:

```cpp
bool hasDuplicates(const vector<int>& nums) {
  unordered_set<int> seen;

  for (int num : nums) {
    if (seen.count(num) > 0) {
      return true;
    }
    seen.insert(num);
  }

  // No duplicates found
  return false;
}
```

17. Recursion

Recursion is a powerful technique in programming where a function calls itself to solve smaller instances of a larger problem. It simplifies the implementation of solutions for problems that are naturally recursive, such as tree traversals, factorial calculation, Fibonacci numbers, and certain algorithmic challenges commonly encountered in coding interviews.

A recursive function has two primary components:

Base Case: A condition that stops the recursion by providing a direct, non-recursive solution to the smallest version of the problem.

Recursive Case: The portion of the function where it calls itself with a smaller or simpler problem.

Example 1: Factorial Calculation

```
int factorial(int n) {
  // Base case
  if (n <= 1)
    return 1;
  // Recursive case
  return n * factorial(n - 1);
}
```

Example 2: Fibonacci Sequence

```
int fibonacci(int n) {
  // Base case
  if (n <= 1)
    return n;

  // Recursive case
  return fibonacci(n - 1) +
         fibonacci(n - 2);
}
```

Advantages of Recursion

Simplicity: Many problems are easier and more intuitive to express recursively.

Clarity: Recursive code is often shorter and clearer, closely resembling mathematical or logical definitions.

Drawbacks of Recursion

Stack Overflow Risk: Deep recursion can exhaust the program stack, causing stack overflow errors.

Performance Overhead: Recursive functions have overhead due to multiple function calls, which can impact performance.

Memoization

As we mentioned in the Maps chapter, we can avoid repeating computations for values we have already obtained by storing each computed value in a map.

The following code is an optimized version of the recursive Fibonacci sequence implementation.

```cpp
unordered_map<int, int> memo;

int fibonacci(int n) {
  // Base case
  if (n <= 1)
    return n;

  if (memo.find(n) != memo.end())
    return memo[n];

  // Store the result
  memo[n] = fibonacci(n - 1) +
            fibonacci(n - 2);
  return memo[n];
}
```

Practical Tips for Coding Interviews

- Clearly identify base cases to prevent infinite loops and stack overflow errors.
- You can optimize recursion by avoiding repeated computations by using the **memoization** technique
- Consider iterative solutions when recursion overhead or stack limitations are concerns.

When to Use Recursion

In the context of coding interviews, recursion is commonly used for problems involving traversal or pathfinding in hierarchical data structures such as trees and graphs.

18. Trees

Trees are hierarchical data structures. They consist of connected nodes, with one node called the root serving as the starting point, as it has no parent node. Trees provide efficient ways to organize, store, and access data, particularly when hierarchical relationships are required.

Tree Terminology

Node: A fundamental unit containing data and pointers to child nodes.

Root: The topmost node of a tree.

Child: A node directly connected to another node when moving away from the root.

Parent: A node directly connected to another node when moving towards the root.

Leaf: A node without any children.

Depth: Length of the path from the root to a given node.

Height: Length of the longest path from a given node to a leaf.

Types of Trees

Binary Tree: A tree where each node has up to two children.

Binary Search Tree (BST): A binary tree in which each node's left child is smaller and each right child is greater than the node itself.

Balanced Binary Tree: Ensures height remains logarithmic (O(log n)) for efficient operations.

Binary Tree Implementation in C++

First, let's define the structure of our tree nodes in the following listing:

```cpp
struct TreeNode {
    int value;
    TreeNode* left;
    TreeNode* right;

    TreeNode(int val) : value(val),
                        left(nullptr),
                        right(nullptr)
{}
};
```

Tree Traversals Orders

Pre-order (Root → Left → Right): Used to create a copy of the tree.

In-order (Left → Root → Right): Used in binary search trees to retrieve elements in sorted order.

Post-order (Left → Right → Root): Used to delete or free nodes safely.

Level-order (Breadth-first): Visits nodes level by level.

Example: Pre-order Traversal

```cpp
void preOrderTraversal(TreeNode* root) {
  if (root == nullptr)
    return;
  // Visit the current node
  cout << root->value << " ";

  // Traverse left subtree
  preOrderTraversal(root->left);

  // Traverse right subtree
  preOrderTraversal(root->right);
}
```

Example: In-order Traversal

```cpp
void inorderTraversal(TreeNode* root)
{
  if (root == nullptr)
    return;

  inorderTraversal(root->left);
  cout << root->value << " ";
  inorderTraversal(root->right);
}
```

Example: Post-order Traversal

```cpp
void postOrder(TreeNode* root) {
  if (root == nullptr)
    return;

  // Traverse left subtree
  postOrder(root->left);

  // Traverse right subtree
  postOrder(root->right);

  // Visit the current node
  cout << root->value << " ";
}
```

Example: Level-order Traversal

```cpp
void levelOrder(TreeNode* root) {
  if (root == nullptr)
    return;

  queue<TreeNode*> q;
  q.push(root);

  while (!q.empty()) {
    TreeNode* current = q.front();
    q.pop();

    cout << current->value << " ";

    if (current->left)
      q.push(current->left);
    if (current->right)
      q.push(current->right);
  }
}
```

Tree Time Complexity

- Traversals: O(n)
- Insertions, Deletions, Searches in a balanced binary search tree: O(log n) on average.

Inverting a Binary Tree

One well-known interview problem is inverting a binary tree. It is often cited by critics who argue that coding interviews are flawed.

In 2015, Max Howell, the creator of the Homebrew package manager for macOS, shared on social media his disappointment after failing a job interview at Google because he was unable to invert a binary tree.

This is what Max Howell (@mxcl) posted on X on June 10, 2015: *"Google: 90% of our engineers use the software you wrote (Homebrew), but you can't invert a binary tree on a whiteboard…"*

I would not blame either the interviews per se or highly skilled professionals like Max on this recurring issue. My point is that, as a software engineer, it is valuable to have a solid grasp of fundamental data structures and algorithmic concepts, such as those covered in this book. This knowledge is useful not only for passing coding interviews but also for encouraging creative problem-solving and thinking outside of the box. In this context, thinking outside the box means avoiding reliance on third-party libraries for every task, including trivial ones, and being able to create efficient solutions.

Now that you know the basic concept of a tree, and the traversal orders, using the same tree structure that we have been using during this chapter we can write a function that inverts a binary tree, recursively in less than 10 lines of code, as follows:

```cpp
void invert(TreeNode* node) {
  if (node != nullptr) {
    swap(node->left, node->right);
    invert(node->left);
    invert(node->right);
  }
}
```

Figure 18.1 illustrates an input binary tree on the left and its inverted output on the right.

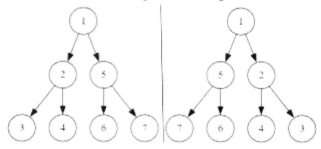

Figure 18.1 Inverted binary tree.

Searching for a Node in a Balanced Binary Tree

In a balanced binary tree, we can efficiently search for a given value in a manner similar to the binary search demonstrated in the Arrays chapter as it is demonstrated in the following code listing.

```cpp
bool search(TreeNode* root, int key) {
    if (root == nullptr)
        return false;
    if (key == root->value)
        return true;
    if (key < root->value)
        return search(root->left, key);
    else
        return search(root->right, key);
}
```

19. Graphs

Graphs consist of vertices connected by edges.

Graph Terminology

Vertex: Each element of the graph.

Edge: Connection between two vertices.

Adjacent: Vertices directly connected by an edge.

Degree: Number of edges connected to a vertex.

Path: Sequence of vertices connected by edges.

Cycle: A path where the start and end vertices are the same.

Types of Graphs

Directed Graphs: Edges have direction, indicating a one-way connection.

Undirected Graphs: Edges do not have a specific direction; connections are bidirectional.

Weighted Graphs: Edges have weights representing costs, distances, or capacities.

Directed Weighted Graph Example:

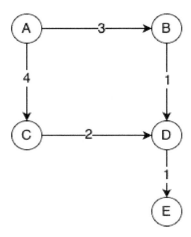

Figure 19.1: A directed weighted graph.

In the directed, weighted graph shown in Figure 19.1, there are two possible paths from A to E: A → C → D → E and A → B → D → E. By adding the weights of the edges, we can determine that the shortest path is A → B → D → E.

Here is the breakdown. Paths from A to E:

1. **A → C → D → E**

   - A to C: 4

   - C to D: 2

   - D to E: 1

   - **Total cost: 4 + 2 + 1 = 7**

2. **A → B → D → E**

   - A to B: 3

   - B to D: 1

   - D to E: 1

   - **Total cost: 3 + 1 + 1 = 5**

Programmatic Graph Representation

Graphs are commonly represented in one of these two ways:

Adjacency Matrix

Adjacency matrices are two-dimensional Boolean arrays that indicate the presence or absence of edges. In an adjacency matrix, both the columns and rows represent all the vertices of the graph, and their intersection determines whether the vertices are directly connected by an edge.

It is not recommended to use adjacency matrices for graph traversal problems, because, in this scenario they are inefficient, both space and time complexity wise. This type of matrix has a space and traversal time complexity of $O(V^2)$.

The only advantage of the adjacency matrix over the adjacency list is that they provide a constant time complexity $O(1)$ for edge existence checking, outperforming the linear $O(N)$ time complexity of the same operation on adjacency lists.

Adjacency List

A list of all the edges of a given vertex. In this approach, each vertex contains a list of edges. This approach provides both space and traversal time complexity of $O(V+E)$, where V stands for Vertices and E for edges.

The decision on whether to represent adjacency with matrices or lists depends on the requirements of the problem.

Adjacency List Example:

```
struct Edge;

struct Vertex {
  string name;
  vector<Edge> edges;

  Vertex(const string& n) : name(n) {}

  void addEdge(Vertex* to, int weight) {
    edges.emplace_back(this, to, weight);
  }
};

struct Edge {
  Vertex* from;
  Vertex* to;
  int weight;

  Edge(Vertex* f, Vertex* t, int w) :
                          from(f),
                          to(t),
                          weight(w) {}
};
```

Common Graph Algorithms

Breadth-First Search (BFS): Explores nodes level by level, used to find the shortest path in unweighted graphs.

Depth-First Search (DFS): Explores as far as possible along branches before backtracking, used to detect cycles, connectivity and path existence.

Example: Breadth-First Graph Traversal

```cpp
void BFS(Vertex* start) {
  queue<Vertex*> q;
  unordered_set<Vertex*> visited;
  q.push(start);
  visited.insert(start);

  while (!q.empty()) {
    Vertex* current = q.front();
    q.pop();
    cout << "Visited: " << current->name << "\n";

    for (const auto& edge : current->edges) {
      if (visited.find(edge.to) ==
                         visited.end()) {
        visited.insert(edge.to);
        q.push(edge.to);
      }
    }
  }
}
```

Example: Depth First Graph Traversal

```cpp
void DFS(Vertex* start,
         unordered_set<Vertex*>& visited) {

  if (visited.find(start) != visited.end()) {
    return;
  }

  cout << "Visited: " << start->name << "\n";
  visited.insert(start);

  for (const auto& edge : start->edges) {
    DFS(edge.to, visited);
  }
}
```

Finding if a Path Exists Between Two Vertices

If we want to determine whether a path exists between two given vertices, both breadth-first search (BFS) and depth-first search (DFS) approaches will work. If you know beforehand that the input graph is wide, a BFS would be the best choice. On the other hand, if you expect the graph to be deep, DFS would likely be more efficient.

In cases where the average or most likely structure of the graph is unknown, BFS and DFS will offer roughly the same time complexity in practice.

100

However, I recommend using a depth-first search (DFS) approach, as it is easier to implement and typically requires fewer lines of code when written recursively. This can save valuable time during a coding interview.

Steps:

1. Start from the source node.
2. Mark the node as visited.
3. Recursively explore all adjacent unvisited nodes.
4. If the destination node is found, a path exists.

Depth-First Search Example:

```
unordered_set<Vertex*> visited;

bool pathExists(Vertex* current,
                Vertex* destination) {
  if (current == destination) {
    return true;
  }

  visited.insert(current);

  for (const Edge& edge : current->edges) {
    if (visited.find(edge.to) == visited.end()) {
      if (pathExists(edge.to, destination)) {
        return true;
      }
    }
  }

  return false;
}
```

Finding the Shortest Path Between Two Vertices of an Unweighted Graph

For finding the shortest path between two vertices in an unweighted graph, a breadth-first search (BFS) approach is preferred because it searches all node neighbors before moving deeper.

The following code shows a simple BFS approach for finding the shortest path for an unweighted graph:

```cpp
unordered_set<Vertex*> visited;
vector<Vertex*> getShortestPath(
                       Vertex* source,
                       Vertex* destination) {

  if (source == nullptr ||
      destination == nullptr)
    return {};
  unordered_map<Vertex*, Vertex*> parent;
  unordered_set<Vertex*> visited;
  queue<Vertex*> q;
  q.push(source);
  visited.insert(source);
  parent[source] = nullptr;

  while (!q.empty()) {
    Vertex* current = q.front();
    q.pop();

    if (current == destination) {
      break;
    }

    for (const Edge& edge : current->edges) {
      if (visited.find(edge.to) ==
          visited.end()) {
        visited.insert(edge.to);
        parent[edge.to] = current;
        q.push(edge.to);
      }
    }
  }
```

```
  if (visited.find(destination) ==
      visited.end()) {
    return {};
  }

  vector<Vertex*> path;
  for (Vertex* at = destination;
               at != nullptr;
               at = parent[at]) {
    path.push_back(at);
  }

  reverse(path.begin(), path.end());
  return path;
}
```

Dijkstra's Algorithm

Dijkstra's algorithm is widely used to find the shortest path between two vertices in a weighted graph.

It is worth to add the disclaimer stating that this algorithm would only work if all weights are non-negative, but since this book is focused on the essential of what you need for passing the coding interview we are just going to cover Dijkstra algorithm because chances are that the problem that require you to find the shortest path within a weighted graph will be solvable using Dijkstra's algorithm.

Steps:

1. Use a priority queue to visit the closest vertex.
2. Update distances to adjacent vertices if a shorter path is found.
3. Repeat until the destination node is visited or the queue is empty.

Implementation:

```
vector<Vertex*> dijkstra(Vertex* start,
                         Vertex* end) {

  unordered_map<Vertex*, int> distances;
  unordered_map<Vertex*, Vertex*> previous;
```

```cpp
priority_queue< pair<int, Vertex*>,
            vector<pair<int, Vertex*>>,
            greater<>> pq;

vector<Vertex*> path;

distances[start] = 0;
pq.push({0, start});

while (!pq.empty()) {
  int currentDist = pq.top().first;
  Vertex* currentVertex = pq.top().second;
  pq.pop();

  if (currentVertex == end)
    break;

  if (distances.find(currentVertex) !=
                    distances.end() &&
      currentDist > distances[currentVertex])
    continue;

  for (const Edge& edge:currentVertex->edges){
    int newDist =
          distances[currentVertex] +
          edge.weight;
    if (distances.find(edge.to) ==
        distances.end() ||
        newDist < distances[edge.to]) {
      distances[edge.to] = newDist;
      previous[edge.to] = currentVertex;
      pq.push({newDist, edge.to});
    }
```

```cpp
    }
  }

  if (distances.find(end) == distances.end()) {
    return path;  // No path exists
  }

  // Reconstruct the shortest path
  for (Vertex* at = end;
              at != nullptr;
              at = previous[at]) {
    path.push_back(at);
  }
  reverse(path.begin(), path.end());
  return path;
}
```

Let's now explain this implementation more thoroughly.

Step 1: Initialize data structures

```cpp
unordered_map<Vertex*, int> distances;
unordered_map<Vertex*, Vertex*> previous;
priority_queue<pair<int, Vertex*>,
               vector<pair<int, Vertex*>>,
               greater<>> pq;
vector<Vertex*> path;
```

distances: stores the **shortest known distance** from *start* to each vertex.

previous: tracks the **previous vertex** on the shortest path for each visited vertex.

pq: a **priority queue** to get the vertex with the **lowest tentative distance** next.

path: will contain the final shortest path (if found).

Step 2: Start with the source node

```
distances[start] = 0;
pq.push({0, start});
```

1. Set the starting vertex distance to *0* because it is the origin.

2. Push the start vertex into the priority queue with priority *0*.

Step 3: Main loop (Dijkstra's Algorithm)

Runs while there are vertices left to process.

```
while (!pq.empty()) {
    ...
}
```

Inside the loop:

Step 3.1: Get the vertex with the smallest distance

```
int currentDist = pq.top().first;
Vertex* currentVertex =
pq.top().second;
pq.pop();
```

Pop the vertex with the **smallest distance** from the priority queue.

Step 3.2: Early exit if reached the destination

```
if (currentVertex == end)
  break;
```

If the current vertex is the end, we found the shortest path and can stop early.

Step 3.3: Skip if we already found a shorter path

```
if (distances.find(currentVertex) !=
    distances.end() &&
    currentDist >
distances[currentVertex])
  continue;
```

Skip if there's already a shorter known path to currentVertex.

Step 3.4: Explore neighboring vertices

```cpp
for (const Edge& edge : currentVertex->edges)
{
   ...
}
```

Iterate over all edges connected to the current vertex.

Step 3.4.1: Compute distance through current vertex

```cpp
int newDist = distances[currentVertex] +
                  edge.weight;
```

newDist is the total distance from *start* to *edge.to* via *currentVertex*.

Step 3.4.2: Update if shorter path is found

```
if (distances.find(edge.to) ==
            distances.end() ||
            newDist < distances[edge.to]) {
  distances[edge.to] = newDist;
  previous[edge.to] = currentVertex;
  pq.push({newDist, edge.to});
}
```

If this is the first time visiting *edge.to*, or if we found a shorter path to it:

1. Update its distance.
2. Record the previous vertex.
3. Add it to the priority queue for further exploration.

Step 4: Check if a path was found

```
if (distances.find(end) == distances.end()){
  return path;
}
```

If the destination *end* vertex wasn't reached, return an **empty path**.

Step 5: Reconstruct the path

```
for (Vertex* at = end;
            at != nullptr;
            at = previous[at]) {
  path.push_back(at);
}
reverse(path.begin(), path.end());
return path;
```

1. Start from the *end* vertex and walk backward using the *previous* map.

2. Push each vertex onto the *path* array.

3. The path is built in reverse, so it's reversed before returning.

Complexity Summary:

- **Time complexity:**, $O((V + E) \log V)$ where V is the number of vertices, and E is the number of edges.
- **Space complexity**: $O(V + E)$ due to storing distances, previous vertices, and the priority queue.

Practical Tips for Coding Interviews

- Unless the main problem is related to detecting if an edge between two vertices exist, use an adjacency list for representing edges.
- Be familiar with core algorithms like BFS and DFS, as they are frequently used in solving graph-based problems.
- If the problem only requests you to find the existence of a path between vertices use a Depth First Search approach.
- If a problem asks you to find the shortest path between vertices in an unweighted graph, use a Breadth-First Search (BFS) approach.
- Practice the Dijkstra algorithm for finding the shortest path of a weighted graph.
- Know the complexities:
  - Adjacency List Traversal: $O(V + E)$
  - Adjacency Matrix Traversal: $O(V^2)$
  - Find the shortest path between two given vertices of a unweighted graph $O(V + E)$
  - Find the shortest path between two given vertices of a weighted graph $O((V + E) \log V)$

20. Closing Words

You've reached the end of The Coding Interview Prep Handbook. This journey has been both challenging and rewarding, much like the path of becoming a successful software engineer itself. By working through each chapter, you've gained not only knowledge but also confidence and clarity about coding interviews, data structures, algorithms, and the broader context of a software engineering career.

Remember, mastering coding interviews is as much about understanding the underlying principles as it is about practice. The hours you've invested in studying the topics covered in this handbook have equipped you with invaluable problem-solving skills that go beyond mere interview preparation. These skills lay a strong foundation for your entire programming career.

Coding interviews, though sometimes daunting, serve as gateways rather than barriers. They are opportunities to demonstrate your analytical thinking, creativity, persistence, and ability to communicate effectively, qualities that distinguish great engineers from good ones. Embrace each interview as a chance to learn and grow, regardless of the immediate outcome.

As technology continues to evolve rapidly, especially with advancements like AI, your ability to adapt, learn continuously, and solve new problems will define your success. Approach your career with curiosity, passion, and resilience. Never stop coding, exploring, or challenging yourself.

As mentioned in the first part of this book, I wrote it with the intention of making it a concise handbook, removing all the fat and leaving only the steak. Of course, there are topics not covered here that you might find in other, more extensive books on the subject. This leads us to the final lesson of this book: focus. Don't get overwhelmed by all the details and every possible edge case that could arise during your coding interviews. Instead, focus on mastering the core concepts, and keep practicing in coding problem solving platforms like LeetCode. Have fun, and enjoy the adventure of this wonderful career you've chosen.

Thank you for allowing this handbook to be part of your journey. Now, take a deep breath, trust your preparation, and go forward confidently. Your next big opportunity is waiting for you.

If you enjoyed this book, please consider leaving us a review on Amazon.

www.ingramcontent.com/pod-product-compliance
Lightning Source LLC
LaVergne TN
LVHW022352060326
832902LV00022B/4390